AMERICAN BIBLE SOCIETY

READ and LEARN™

5-Minute Bible Stories

Faith-Filled Stories
to Read Aloud

Retold by Amy Parker
Illustrated by Walter Carzon

ABS logo is a registered trademark of American Bible Society,
101 North Independence Mall East, FL 8, Philadelphia, PA 19106-2112.
Used by permission.

ISBN: 978-1-5461-8503-1

10 9 8 7 6 5 4 3 2 1   25 26 27 28 29

Art direction by Paul W. Banks
Design by Kay Petronio

Printed in China 84
5-Minute Bible Stories was originally published under the title
Five-Minute Bedtime Bible Stories.

This edition first printing, June 2025.

Scholastic Inc., 557 Broadway, New York, NY 10012

Scholastic UK, Ltd., No 1 London Bridge, London SE1 9BG

Scholastic LTD, Unit 89E, Lagan Road,
Dublin Industrial Estate, Glasnevin, Dublin 11 HP5F

Little
Shepherd®
BOOKS

Table of Contents

Trees, Bees, You, and Me! 1

A Big, Big Boat for a Big, Big Flood 17

Walls of Water 35

A Boy, a Giant, and an Almighty God 49

The Brave Young Queen 65

Safe in the Lions' Den 85

A Child Is Born 101

Seeds and Storms 117

One Little Lunch 133

Now I See 147

Who Is My Neighbor? 163

Jesus Is Alive! 177

Trees, Bees, You, and Me!

Genesis 1–2

In the beginning, before there was anything, God created the earth and the heavens around the earth. Then God decided to fill the earth with beautiful and amazing things.

God said, "Let there be light." With those four words, light filled the earth. God made daytime and nighttime, creating the very first day.

And God was just getting started.

On the second day, God said, "Let the sky be separated from the earth." And it happened as God said. The waters of the sky separated from the waters of the earth. And the sky spread out far and wide above the world.

On the third day, God pulled all of the water on the earth together to make oceans and lakes, rivers and creeks. He left wide spaces of dry land, too. Then God said, "Let there be lots of plants on the land—*every kind of plant*! Let there be plants with seeds and trees with fruit, so that even more plants and trees can grow from *their* seeds and *their* fruit."

And that's just what happened.

Daisies and daffodils jumped up from the soil! Lilies and lilacs bloomed big and beautiful! Trees stretched out their bright green leaves, reaching for the sun. Apples burst forth in red and green and yellow. Tall grasses, reeds, and wheat waved in the new, sweet-smelling breeze.

God had created the earth and the skies, daytime and nighttime, and trees and plants, too. And God saw that it was good.

But God wasn't finished yet!

On the fourth day, God said, "Let there be a big, bright light for the day. And let there be a smaller light for the night."

And that's just what happened.

He gave us the shining sun to warm our days. And he gave us the shimmery moon and twinkly stars to brighten our nights.

As the stars faded and the sun rose on the fifth day, God brought the oceans and the skies to life. "Let the oceans be filled with all sorts of creatures!" he said. "And let the skies be filled with birds of every kind!"

And that's just what happened.

Up splashed the dolphins and the minnows and the big blue whales! The waters wriggled with curious new creatures. The skies came alive with birds in flight—herons and hummingbirds, pigeons and parrots, cardinals and kookaburras!

God was very pleased. He blessed the fish and the birds. He told them, "Multiply and fill the earth!"

On the sixth day, God created the animals—every kind
of animal. Huge and loud, quiet and gentle, spiky and fuzzy,
smelly and beautiful—God created them all! Lions roared,
mice squeaked, and kittens meowed.

The earth was alive with brand-new sights and sounds and smells.

God was so pleased. But still, he created even more.

From the dust of the earth, God formed the very first man. God himself breathed life into the man. And that man became the first human ever to live on this earth. God named him Adam and placed him in a garden called Eden. The garden was full of life.

"You will rule over all these creatures," God told Adam, "the birds, the fish, and the animals, too."

Adam named them all—aardvarks, blue jays, catfish—until each of the creatures had its own name. While he was naming them, Adam noticed something. He saw that the animals had other animals to play with. The birds had other birds to sing with. And the fish had other fish that swam around just like them.

But Adam was alone. He was the only human in the whole wide world.

Of course, God was always with Adam. But God knew that Adam wanted someone who was a human, like him, to share his life with.

So, after creating plants and animals and man, God *still* wasn't finished.

"I will make another person," God said. "The perfect match for the man!" So God put Adam into a deep, deep sleep and took out one of Adam's ribs. Then, just as God had created a man from nothing but dust, he created a woman using only the rib from a man.

When Adam saw the woman, he said, "At last! Someone like me." Adam now had someone to talk to and someone to love. He named his beautiful wife Eve.

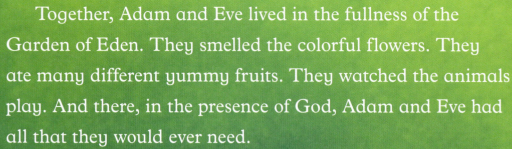

Together, Adam and Eve lived in the fullness of the Garden of Eden. They smelled the colorful flowers. They ate many different yummy fruits. They watched the animals play. And there, in the presence of God, Adam and Eve had all that they would ever need.

On the seventh day, God looked at the earth and the heavens, the sun and the stars, the plants, the animals, and the people. He looked at *all* of the amazing things that he had created. And God saw that it was all so good.

Then on that day, God—the almighty, all-knowing, and all-powerful—took a good, long rest.

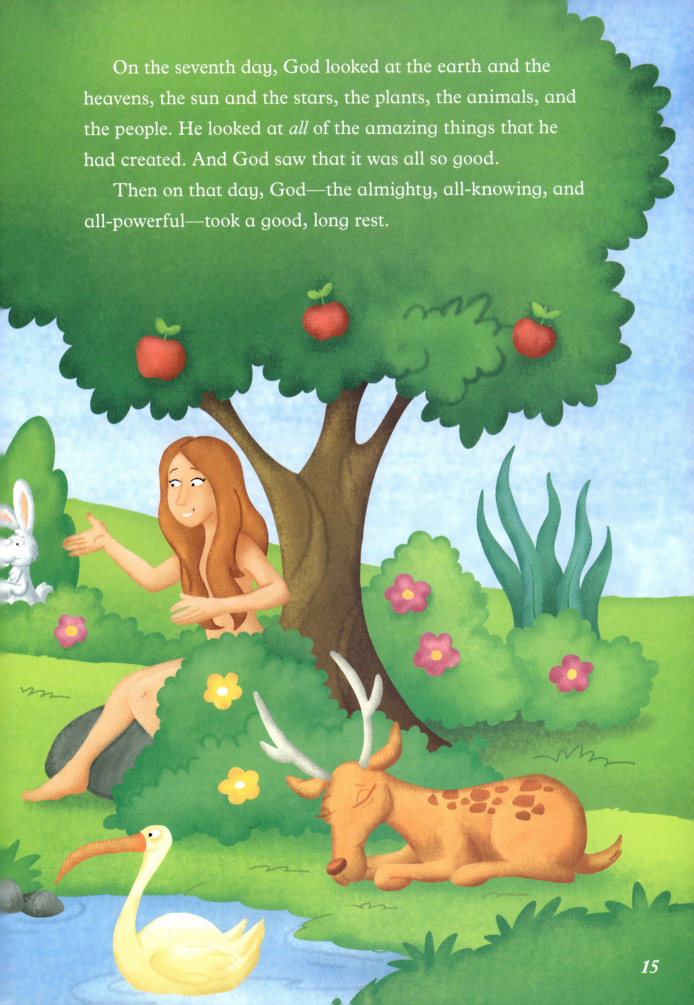

A Big, Big Boat for a Big, Big Flood

Genesis 6–9

When God created the world, he had filled it with beautiful and amazing things. Hundreds of years later, the people of the world had forgotten about God. But

God was still watching over them. When he looked at the world, the people made him very sad. It seemed to God as if everyone had become bad—well, everyone except for a man named Noah.

When God looked down at Noah, he was pleased with what he saw. God saw that Noah listened to him. He saw that Noah always tried to do what was right.

So one day, God spoke to Noah. God said, "I am going to wash the whole world in a flood. But I want you and your wife, your sons and their wives to be safe."

God told Noah to build a big, big boat, called an ark.
And he told him exactly how to build it: "Make it 450 feet
long, 75 feet wide, and 45 feet high. Make lots of rooms on
three different levels. Build it out of wood. Then cover the
whole thing—inside and out—with tar to keep the water out."

Noah did everything that God told him to do.

Day after day, Noah and his sons worked on the ark. He didn't mind the hard work. Other people thought he was crazy for building such a big boat. But Noah didn't care what everyone thought. Noah knew that God had told him to build an ark. So that's exactly what Noah was doing.

God had also told Noah, "When you go into the ark, take with you a pair of all the living creatures—animals and birds and even the creatures that crawl on the ground. They will come to you so that you can keep them alive. And be sure to take lots of different kinds of plants and food, enough for you and all the animals to eat."

Noah did everything that God told him to do.
As the ark took shape, animals of every kind found their
way to Noah. Cows and camels, doves and ducks,
snakes and skunks all gathered around the man
whom God had chosen to keep them safe.

When the time came, God said to Noah, "Go into the ark and take all of the animals with you. I am sending rain for forty days and forty nights. This rain will flood the earth, wiping it clean."

So Noah stepped into the ark with his family. With them came the pairs of animals, two by two.

The day that they entered the boat, the floods came, just as God had said. The skies opened up and huge pounding raindrops fell to the ground. The lakes and rivers and oceans burst open. Water spilled onto the land.

Noah's ark began to float. His family and all the animals were safe inside the ark.

For forty days, the rain fell, and the water continued to rise. The water rose higher and higher until Noah's ark floated above the highest mountains on earth. For months and months, waves crashed over the earth. And for months and months, Noah and his family and all the animals safely rocked on the waves.

Then God looked down on the ark and on everyone inside. He knew they had been in there with all the sounds and smells of the animals for a long, long time. So God decided it was time for the flood to be over. He sent a strong, howling wind across the earth, and the rains stopped. The water went down, down, down until finally the ark came to rest on top of a mountain.

The mountaintop was still surrounded by water. So Noah decided to send a bird to fly out over the water. If the bird returned to him, Noah would know that there was no grass or trees for the bird to land on. So Noah opened a window of the ark and sent out a dove. But the dove found no place to rest. It soon returned to the ark.

After seven more days, Noah sent out the dove again. This time, the dove came back with an olive leaf in its beak.

When Noah saw the leaf, he knew that the water had gone down. He knew that trees and plants had begun to grow again on land. Noah was overjoyed.

Now that the earth was dry, God spoke to Noah. He said, "Noah, it is time to leave the ark. Bring out all of the animals—the blue jays and blackbirds, hyenas and hippos, the toads and the turtles, too. Send them out into the world to multiply and fill the earth again."

Noah did everything that God told him to do.

When everyone was on dry land again, Noah thanked God. Noah thanked God for keeping him, his family, and all of the animals safe.

God blessed Noah's family. He told them, "Be fruitful. Fill the earth with good people again."

Then God made a promise. "Never again will I send a flood over all the earth." With these words, God put a rainbow in the sky.

The bright colors of the rainbow—red, orange, yellow, green, blue, indigo, and violet—curved above the clouds. It was a glistening reminder of God's promise to the world.

Every time Noah and his family saw the rainbow in the clouds, they remembered God's promise. And they remembered how God had kept them safe during the big, big flood.

Walls
of Water

Exodus 1–14

Hundreds of years after the big flood, there lived a great man named Abraham. Abraham obeyed and honored God in all that he did. God told Abraham, "I will always be your God. And your family will always be my people." From then on, Abraham's family, the Hebrews, were known as God's people.

The Hebrews lived in Egypt. They were forced to work for a mean king called Pharaoh. Pharaoh ruled over the Hebrews. But he was also afraid of the Hebrews. He was afraid that if they kept having more children, there would be enough Hebrews to take over Egypt. He wanted to stop the Hebrew families from getting bigger. So Pharaoh created a new rule: "Hebrew families are not allowed to have any more baby boys."

Then one day, an adorable baby boy was born to a Hebrew family. The mother loved her son very much, but she was scared. If Pharaoh found her baby, he would take the baby away. The mother hid the baby inside her home. The baby's big sister, Miriam, tried to help keep him quiet and out of sight. But his cries and coos grew louder. And the mother realized that she could no longer keep her baby safe at home.

The mother had to find another way to protect him. She made a tightly woven basket and painted it with tar to keep water out. Then she tucked her baby boy snugly inside the basket. Miriam followed her mother to the Nile River. Kneeling by the riverbank, the mother placed the basket in the reeds just beyond the bank. She gave her son a good-bye kiss. Then the mother hid her tears and snuck away.

Miriam stayed to see what would happen to her baby brother. She heard voices. She peered down the river as Pharaoh's daughter stepped into the river to bathe. The princess stood only a few feet from where Miriam's baby brother rocked in the water.

"Look!" the princess cried to one of her servants. "Please bring that basket to me."

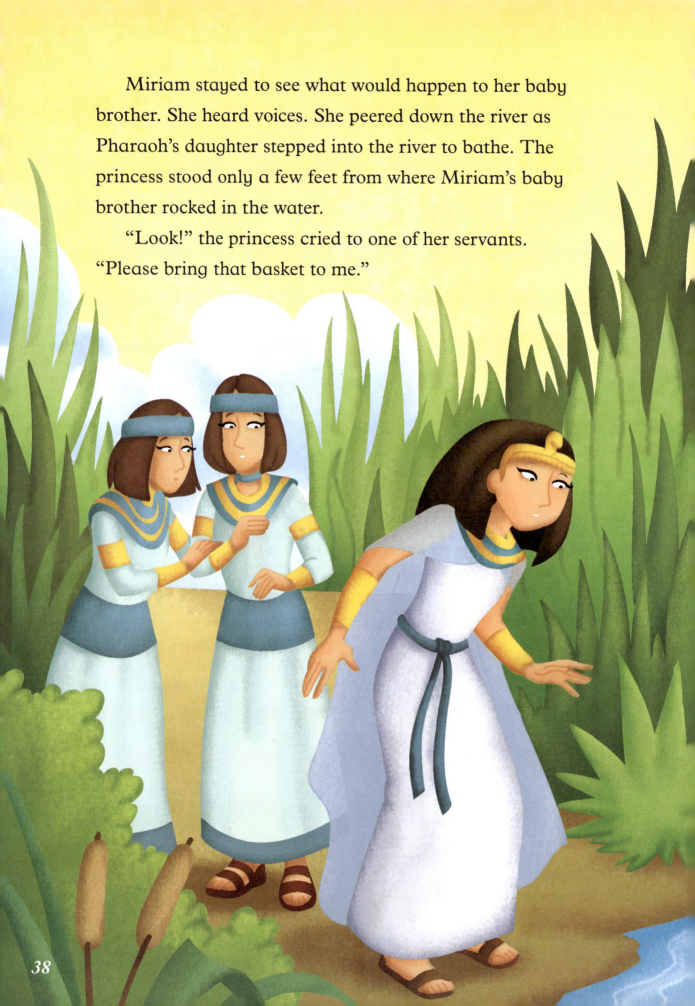

Miriam held her breath as she watched the servant pick up the basket and hand it to the princess. The princess cradled the baby boy close to her. "One of the Hebrews must have hidden her baby boy here," the princess said. "I want to keep him safe. But I have no way to care for a baby this young."

At that moment, brave Miriam ran up to the princess. "I can help! I can find a woman to take care of the baby for you!" she said.

The princess agreed, and Miriam ran to find her mother.

"Mother, Mother! You won't believe what has happened!" Miriam called. She explained everything. Together, they quickly made their way back to the riverbank.

"I found this baby in a basket," the princess said to the mother. "But I need someone to care for him until he is old enough to live with me at the palace. I will pay you for your help."

The mother couldn't believe it. Earlier, the mother had kissed her baby boy good-bye. She had thought it was the last time she would ever see him. Now a princess was asking her to care for him again.

Miriam and her mother returned home with the baby. He grew into a walking, talking little boy.

Before long, it was time to return him to the princess.

"Thank you for caring for him," said the princess. "Now I will raise this boy as a prince of Egypt. His name will be Moses." Moses sounded like the Hebrew word for "to draw out." The princess chose this name because she had drawn Moses out of the water.

Moses's mother was sad to say good-bye to her son again. Still, she knew that God had saved her son's life for a reason and that God would keep him safe.

When Moses was all grown-up, there was a new pharaoh in Egypt. The new pharaoh was just as awful as the old one. God saw this, and he called on Moses to free the Hebrews from their mean ruler.

God sent Moses to speak with Pharaoh many times.

"Pharaoh, let God's people go," Moses told him again and again.

But again and again, Pharaoh refused.

God punished Pharaoh and his people for not listening to Moses.

Finally, Pharaoh agreed. "Okay, Moses. I will let the Hebrews go."

But as soon as Moses led the Hebrews out of Egypt, Pharaoh changed his mind.

All of Pharaoh's soldiers came charging toward Moses and the Hebrews. They were trapped! Pharaoh's soldiers rushed at them on one side. And on the other side was the Red Sea. The sea stretched out deep and wide. The people were terrified. Where could they go?

But Moses was not afraid. He knew that God would protect his people. God would find a way to keep them safe.

"Don't be afraid," Moses told them. "The LORD will save us!"

Moses stretched out his hand over the Red Sea. Just then, God sent a strong wind! The wind divided the waters of the sea, pushing up a tall wall of water on each side. For a moment, everyone stood still. They were amazed at the sea parting right in front of them.

Moses led God's people through the dry path God had created. He led them to safety on the other side of the Red Sea.

Then the dry path became a sea once more. Pharaoh's soldiers were washed away.

Once again, God had used the water to save Moses. And God had used Moses to save the Hebrew people.

A Boy, a Giant, and an Almighty God

1 Samuel 17

Deep in the valley, between the hills, two armies met for battle. On one hill, the Philistine army gathered. On the other hill, King Saul stood with God's people, the Israelites. They were all lined up, ready to fight.

Just then, a giant stepped down from among the Philistines. He walked into the valley and stood between the two armies. The giant was more than nine feet tall! He wore a bronze helmet on his head. Scaly bronze armor covered his chest and wrapped around the bottom of his legs. And he carried a long bronze javelin.

"I am the mighty Goliath!" the giant roared. "I will fight for the Philistines!"

Goliath looked at the Israelites up on the hill. "Send someone down to fight me!" he shouted.

The Israelites trembled in fear. They didn't have any men as big as Goliath—not even close! And if the Israelites couldn't defeat the giant, the Philistines would win the battle. The Israelites didn't know what to do so they hid in their camp.

Every morning, Goliath stepped down into the valley and called the Israelites out to fight. "Send someone down to fight me!" the giant shouted.

And every morning, the Israelites listened in fear.

Meanwhile, many miles away, a man named Jesse filled large bags with cheeses and grain. Jesse had eight sons. His seven oldest sons were soldiers for King Saul. They were part of the Israelite army on the hill. His youngest son, David, was a shepherd to their sheep.

"David," Jesse said to his son, "please take this food to your brothers."

So David set out with the food and went to find his brothers.

He found his brothers in the valley, with the rest of King Saul's army. But as soon as he met them, all attention turned to the other side of the valley.

"Come on, you Israelites! Don't you have *anyone* to fight me?" Goliath's voice boomed across the land. David watched the Israelite army scatter and shake with fear.

"Who does this guy think he is?" young David asked the soldiers around him. "He should know better than to threaten the army of the almighty God! I'll fight him!"

"Now, David," his big brother said, "do you think that because you take care of sheep, you can handle a giant? Don't come down here causing trouble! You'll get hurt!"

But other Israelites had heard what David said. And someone ran to tell King Saul that maybe there *was* an Israelite who would face the terrible giant.

King Saul sent for David to see for himself.

"You?" the king asked when David came to him. "*You* are willing to fight Goliath?"

"Yes! I will fight him!" David told the king. "Don't let this giant scare you."

King Saul looked at the boy in front of him. He knew that David wouldn't stand a chance against the growling, rugged, nine-foot-tall warrior waiting in the valley.

"David," King Saul began, "you cannot fight Goliath. He has been a Philistine soldier for many years. He has fought many battles. And you—you are just a boy!"

"I keep watch over my father's sheep," David answered quickly. "And whenever a lion comes for the sheep, I save the sheep right out of the lion's mouth. The same God who has kept me safe from the lion will rescue me from this Philistine giant."

"Very well," the king answered. "May God be with you as you face Goliath."

Then King Saul gave David the best armor that he had—the king's own armor. David put on the armor, but when he tried to walk, he slumped and stumbled.

"I can't wear this," David said, pulling off the helmet. "It's too heavy. And I am not used to wearing armor."

David removed the armor and picked up his shepherd's stick. The king watched in wonder as the boy walked off to face the giant.

At a nearby stream, David carefully chose five smooth stones. He put the stones in his bag. And he went out to meet Goliath.

David walked down into the valley, carrying his sling.
He looked up at the nine-foot-tall giant towering above him.
He gulped. His heart was beating hard in his chest.

Suddenly, Goliath spoke to him. "What am I, a dog?!" he bellowed. "Do you really think you can fight me with that little stick?"

Young David looked the huge warrior in the eye. He spoke up the best he could: "You may come at me with your sword and spear, but I—I come against you in the name of the LORD!"

The giant didn't flinch. Instead, he lunged toward David.

David had to do something—fast! So he rushed toward Goliath. The boy reached into his bag, wrapping his fingers around a cool, smooth stone. He placed the stone into his sling. And he launched the stone up into the air . . .

WHOOSH!
POW!
THUD!
Down came
the giant.

The armies on both sides of the valley froze. No one moved. David stood, looking down at the giant lying on the ground.

Everyone knew that God had helped David win the battle that day. Only God could make a young shepherd boy stand taller than the largest giant in the land.

The Brave Young Queen

Book of Esther

A young girl named Esther lived in a town called Susa. Both of her parents had died and she now lived with her older cousin, Mordecai. Mordecai loved Esther. He raised her as his own daughter, and she grew into a beautiful and kind young woman.

Susa was ruled by King Xerxes. One day, he sent his men throughout the land to search for a young woman who would be his queen . . .

When the king's men met Esther, they saw that she was beautiful and kind. So they invited her to the palace to meet the king.

Esther was nervous. But she was excited to meet the king.
She said good-bye to Mordecai and went to the palace.

Esther was very polite. Everyone she met at the palace loved her. And when the king met Esther, he, too, fell in love with her.

The king had found his queen! Esther felt honored to become queen. She knelt at the king's feet as he placed a jeweled crown upon her head.

Queen Esther lived happily at the palace. And Mordecai came to visit often.

Yet there was one man who was trying to cause trouble for Mordecai. His name was Haman.

Haman was the most important man in the kingdom besides the king himself. Everyone was required to bow to Haman. But when Haman went in and out of the palace gates, Mordecai would not bow. Mordecai was a Jew and would only bow to God.

This made Haman very angry—so angry that he decided he would get rid of Mordecai *and* all of the other Jews, too. But Haman did not know that Queen Esther was a Jew.

Mordecai was horrified by Haman's plans. He ran out into the city, crying loudly.

Esther heard her cousin's cries. And Mordecai soon sent her a message from outside the palace walls . . .

Haman is trying to get rid of us—all of the Jews. Please go and beg King Xerxes to spare our lives. Please, Esther. Maybe God has made you queen for this very time, for this very reason. You are our only hope!

Esther didn't know what to do. No one—not even the queen—was allowed to visit the king without being called by him.

She sent word back to Mordecai: "Gather all of the Jews. Do not eat or drink for three days. And pray, pray, pray. I will do the same. When three days are up, I will go to the king, no matter what."

For three days, Esther prayed. She asked for God's protection for herself and the rest of the Jews. She asked God to guide her as she spoke to the king.

On the third day, Esther walked toward the king's hall. Esther paused for a moment just outside his hall. She wondered, *What will he do? What will he say? What will I say?!*

Then she stepped inside.

The king was happy to see Esther. But as she came into the hall, he could tell that she was upset.

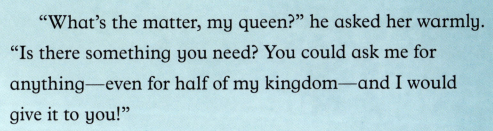

"What's the matter, my queen?" he asked her warmly. "Is there something you need? You could ask me for anything—even for half of my kingdom—and I would give it to you!"

Esther took a deep breath. "Please," she began, "bring Haman to dinner tonight."

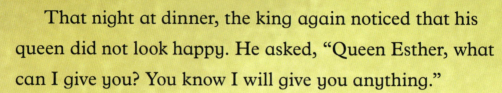

That night at dinner, the king again noticed that his queen did not look happy. He asked, "Queen Esther, what can I give you? You know I will give you anything."

"Well . . ." Esther began. But when she looked at Haman, she lost her courage. "I would like . . . I mean, if the king would like . . . Well, would you and Haman come to dinner again *tomorrow night*?"

The next night, King Xerxes, Queen Esther, and Haman were all seated for dinner again. And again, the king asked what was troubling her.

"What is it, Esther?" the king asked. "Please just say it, and it will be done!"

This time, Esther gathered the courage to ask what she had been waiting to ask all along.

"If I may truly ask for *anything*, Your Majesty," she began, "then please, I ask for *my life* . . . and the lives of my people."

The king's eyes grew wide. "What?! You are in danger?" he demanded. "Where is the man who threatens my queen and her people?!"

"He is right here with us," Esther said. She looked at Haman, then down at her plate. "It is Haman," she said quietly.

The table rumbled as the king jumped from his seat. "Get him out of my sight!" the king called to his men.

Haman was immediately removed from the palace, never to return again.

With Haman gone, Esther and Mordecai told the king the whole story.

The king honored Mordecai. He gave Mordecai Haman's house and Haman's power in the kingdom.

Esther, Mordecai, and their people, the Jews, were saved—all because one young woman had the courage to stand up and make a difference right where God had placed her.

Safe in the Lions' Den

There was a man named Daniel who lived in the kingdom of Babylonia. Daniel had great faith in God.

King Darius was in charge of Babylonia. He had a lot of men who helped him to rule the kingdom. But the king trusted Daniel more than any other man. In fact, he trusted Daniel *so* much that he put him in charge of all the other rulers in the kingdom.

The other rulers didn't like that Daniel was in charge of them.

The rulers wanted to get Daniel in trouble with the king. But they could never catch Daniel doing anything wrong. So they came up with a sneaky plan that was sure to get Daniel into trouble.

One day, they went to speak with the king . . .

"Mighty King Darius, we have come together to ask you to make a new law that honors you," one of the rulers began.

The king nodded.

The ruler continued. "The law shall state that, if someone prays to any god or man other than you, then that man shall be thrown into the den of lions."

One of the rulers handed the written law to the king. "Now sign this law, dear King, to make it official."

King Darius signed the law.

Then the men set out to catch Daniel breaking it. They knew that Daniel was faithful to his God. They knew that, no matter what, Daniel would continue to pray to his God. And they were right.

Daniel had heard about the new law. But he believed that honoring God was much more important than honoring men. So, just as Daniel had done every other day, he went into his room to pray. He was not ashamed of his faith. His windows were wide open for the world to see. Even though it could get him in trouble, Daniel would give thanks to God.

The rulers stood as a group outside Daniel's window. They grinned as they watched Daniel fall to his knees. They smiled as they heard him speak to his God. And they knew that they finally had what they needed to get Daniel in trouble with the king.

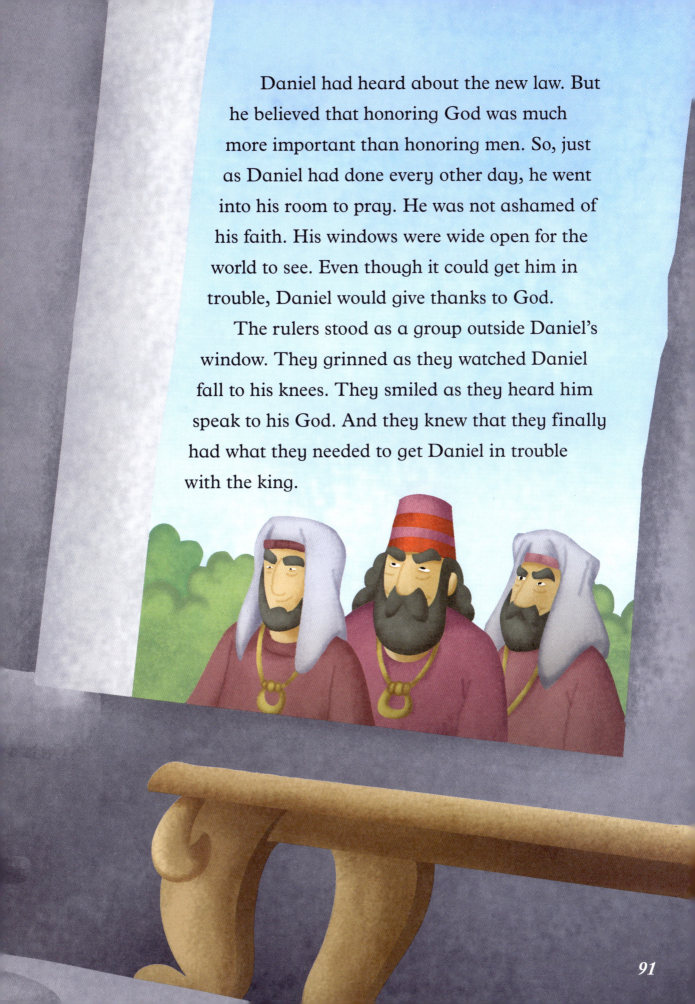

The men rushed off to speak with King Darius.

"Excuse me, King Darius," one of the rulers said, "but didn't you just sign a law saying if someone prayed to anyone but you, that man would be thrown into the lions' den?"

King Darius answered, "Yes, that is true."

"Well . . ." The ruler tried to hide his evil grin. "Daniel doesn't care about you *or* your law. He prays to his God three times a day!"

The king's heart sank. King Darius loved Daniel. He trusted Daniel. And he had never thought that, by signing that law, he would have to send Daniel to the lions' den.

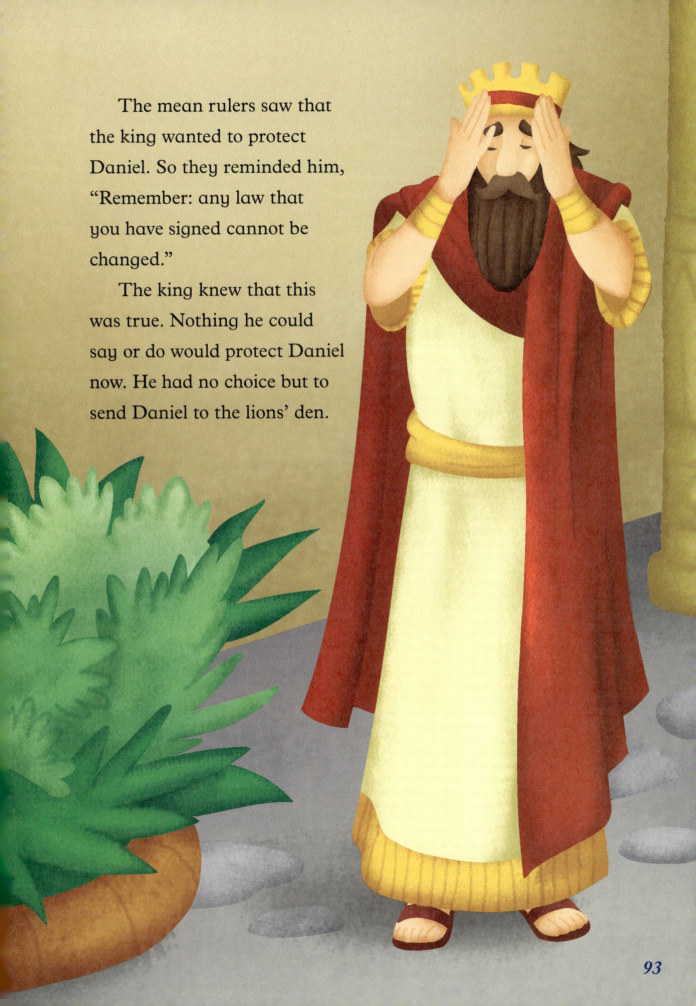

The mean rulers saw that the king wanted to protect Daniel. So they reminded him, "Remember: any law that you have signed cannot be changed."

The king knew that this was true. Nothing he could say or do would protect Daniel now. He had no choice but to send Daniel to the lions' den.

King Darius told his men to go get Daniel and take him to the lions' den. Then the men threw Daniel in with the lions.

The king hurried to the den. He called down to Daniel, "Daniel, may the God that you serve save you from these terrible lions!"

That night at the palace, the king refused to eat. He turned away the musicians who tried to play for him. And he did not sleep at all.

As soon as the first sliver of light fell upon the kingdom, the king jumped up and ran to the lions' den. He yelled into the den, "Daniel, Daniel! Are you okay? Has your God saved you from the lions?"

"Oh yes, King Darius!" came a voice from the lions' den. "God sent an angel to close the lions' mouths. They didn't hurt me at all. I am fine!"

The king was so happy. "Come! Hurry!" he called to his men. "Get Daniel out of the lions' den!"

The men reached into the den. And out climbed Daniel. King Darius ran to him and looked him over. He couldn't believe it. Daniel didn't have a scratch on him.

Daniel had been faithful to God. And God had saved Daniel from the lions' den.

It was then that King Darius decided to punish the rulers who had accused Daniel of disobeying the king's law. He also decided to write a *new* law: "From now on, throughout my kingdom," the king announced, "everyone must honor the God of Daniel."

After that, Daniel continued to serve King Darius. And as always, Daniel continued to worship the one true God.

A Child
Is Born

A young, unmarried woman named Mary lived in a small town called Nazareth. One day, an angel came to visit her.

"Hello, Mary," the angel said.

Mary jumped at the sound of the voice. She turned to see a strange man standing beside her. Well, he *looked* like a man. But his bright white clothes shined like the stars. And his face glowed like the moon. Mary knew that this was no ordinary man.

"I am the angel Gabriel. I have come to tell you that God is with you. He is pleased with you," Gabriel said. "You are blessed above all women."

Mary was stunned. Gabriel was a messenger from God!
And he was right there, speaking to *her*. "Me?" Mary asked.
She looked around, then back at the angel.

Gabriel smiled. "Yes, Mary. Don't be afraid. God wants
me to tell you that you will have a son. You will call him
Jesus. And he will be God's own Son, a Savior for the world."

"But how will I have a child?" Mary asked.

"With God," the angel answered, "everything is possible."

Mary bowed. "I am God's servant. Let this happen just as you say it will."

And soon it did. Mary glowed with joy as she carried within her womb the Son of God.

Then the angel went to see a man named Joseph. Joseph was engaged to be married to Mary at the time. And Gabriel visited him through a dream. . . .

"Joseph, go ahead and take Mary as your wife," Gabriel said. "She is going to have a baby. The baby will be God's Son. His name will be Jesus. And people will call him Emmanuel, because it means 'God is with us.'"

When Joseph awoke, he did as the angel said. Joseph and Mary became husband and wife.

When it was almost time for the baby to be born, the emperor decided that he wanted to count all of the people in his land. He called everyone back to their hometowns to be counted there. Because Joseph was from Bethlehem, he and Mary would have to travel there to be counted. It would be a long and uncomfortable trip for a very pregnant Mary. But she and Joseph had no choice. They would have to make the long journey from Nazareth to Bethlehem.

When Mary and Joseph arrived in Bethlehem, the town was crowded with people who had come home to be counted. Joseph tried to find a room where he and his wife could rest. But all of the rooms were full.

So Mary and Joseph settled into the only room they could find—a room where animals were kept. That night, the *baaa*-ing of the sheep sang Mary and Joseph to sleep.

Soon after, Mary knew it was time for the baby to be born. And under the star of Bethlehem, cows and donkeys and sheep were the first to see the face of the newborn Savior.

Mary wrapped the baby snugly in bands of cloth to keep him warm. Then she laid him on the hay in the animal's feeding box, called a manger.

Joseph smiled as he looked down on the sleeping child. And Mary whispered the name given to her by the angel Gabriel. "Jesus."

That same night, in the fields near Bethlehem, some shepherds were taking care of their sheep when a bright light shined down on them. They were scared, and they hid their faces from the glow.

"Do not be afraid," an angel said to them. "I have good news for you and for *all* people! On this very night, a Savior has been born. You will know him when you see a baby wrapped in cloths, lying in a manger."

Suddenly, the sky filled with more angels! The shepherds didn't move. They didn't speak. They just watched and listened as the angels filled the darkness with praises to God.

"Glory to God!" the angels said. *"Peace and goodness to everyone on earth."*

Then the angels were gone.

The shepherds looked at one another. "Let us go find this baby! Let us go see the Savior!"

The shepherds looked throughout Bethlehem until they found him. They saw a baby wrapped in cloths, lying in a manger—just as the angel had said.

Mary and Joseph were surprised to see the shepherds.

"We—we saw angels," the shepherds explained to Mary and Joseph. "One angel told us that we would find a baby here. And here—here he is! The Savior for the world!"

The shepherds were filled with joy when they saw the baby Jesus. After they had seen him for themselves, they went throughout all of Bethlehem, praising God. They told everyone about the angels and about the baby who would one day be the Savior for the world.

Mary treasured the words of the shepherds and of the angels. She knew in her heart that this was only the beginning. She knew that there would be many more miracles to come for her Son, the Son of God.

Seeds and Storms

Mark 4

When Jesus grew up, he began traveling throughout the countryside. He performed miracles and taught others about God, his heavenly Father.

Jesus had twelve close friends, called disciples, who traveled with him and witnessed the amazing things that he did and said.

Soon, everywhere Jesus went, a large crowd followed to hear what he would say or to see what he would do. Sometimes, Jesus wanted peace and quiet. So he would escape to a mountain or a garden to pray. But he spent most of his days talking with people, sharing God's love, and healing them.

One day, Jesus was teaching on the seashore. The crowd grew so big that Jesus had to climb up into a boat in the sea so that everyone on land could see and hear his message.

Then, as he often did, Jesus told the group a parable—a story that teaches an important lesson.

He told about a farmer who was planting seeds. The farmer scattered the seeds on the ground. But many of the seeds were unable to grow because of where they fell. Some of the seeds fell to the side: Birds swooped in and ate them all up. Some of the seeds fell on rocks, where there was not much soil: The sun dried them up. Some of the seeds fell on thorns: The thorns grew and choked the seedlings so that they could not grow any fruit.

But some of the farmer's seeds fell on good, rich soil. Those seeds grew into lots of plants. Those plants produced lots of fruit. And that fruit produced more seeds that produced more plants that produced more fruit! Those few little seeds—the ones that had fallen on good soil—spread out to make a lot of fruit for a long time to come.

When Jesus finished speaking, the crowd went home. He stepped down onto the shore and was alone with his closest friends. One of them said, "Jesus, I didn't really understand the parable about the seeds. What does it mean?"

"Well," Jesus explained, "the farmer is like a person who spreads the Word of God. Sometimes the Word falls to the side: People hear it but then are tricked by evil.

"Sometimes the Word of God falls on rocks: People hear it, but as soon as something bad happens, they forget it. And sometimes the Word falls on thorns: People hear it, but they let the worries and wants of this world cry louder than God's message. But, my friend, when the Word falls on good ground, people hear the Word. They hold on to it. And they help to spread God's message to many more people."

Jesus's friends then understood the parable of the seeds. They realized how important it was to understand Jesus's teachings and to spread God's Word.

Later that night, Jesus said to his friends, "Let us travel to the other side of the lake." So Jesus and the disciples boarded a boat and set sail.

Before long, a huge storm rolled in. The waves grew and grew until they were crashing over the sides of the boat. The boat began to fill with water! It was rocked and tossed back and forth by the fierce winds and rough waves.

The disciples were scared. They ran left and right, trying to hold on to the sides of the boat. They cried out for help.

One of the disciples went to find Jesus. He was lying in the back of the boat, sleeping peacefully.

"Jesus!" the disciple shouted. "Save us! The boat is going to sink! Don't you care that we are all about to drown?!"

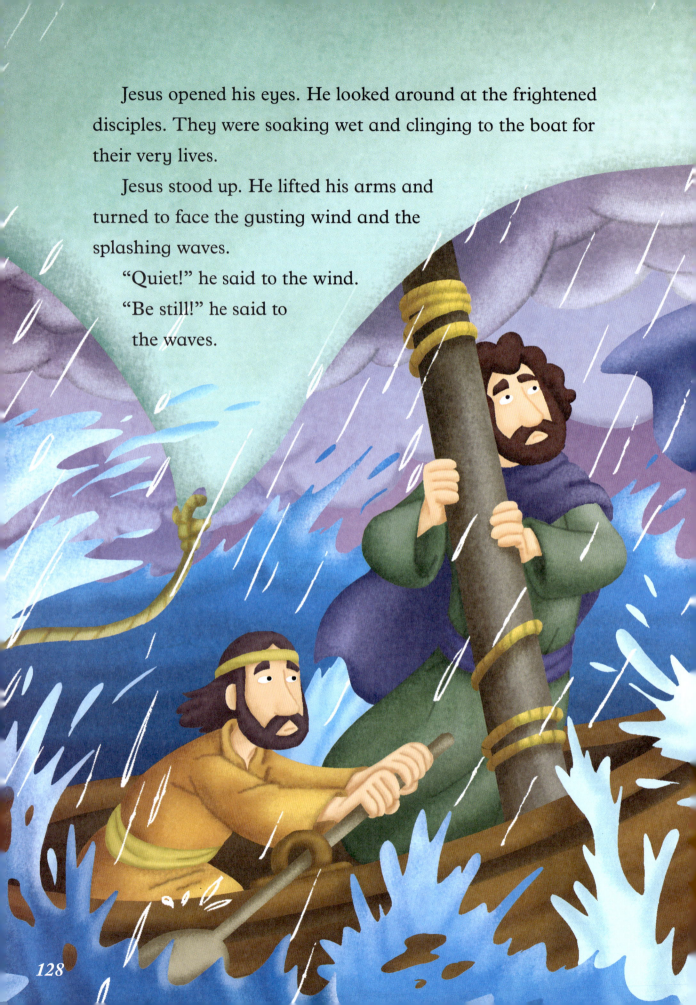

Jesus opened his eyes. He looked around at the frightened disciples. They were soaking wet and clinging to the boat for their very lives.

Jesus stood up. He lifted his arms and turned to face the gusting wind and the splashing waves.

"Quiet!" he said to the wind.

"Be still!" he said to the waves.

The wind stopped.

The waves became calm.

Jesus lowered his arms. He turned to his friends. "Why were you so afraid?" he asked them. "Where is your faith?"

The disciples did not answer him. They were too amazed by how he had stopped the storm and calmed the sea.

As Jesus and his disciples continued their journey across the lake, there was only one question whispered among them:

"Who is this man, that even the wind and the waves obey him?"

But they knew one thing for sure: Jesus was so much more than just a teacher of parables. He had the power to work a miracle, to control the wind and the waves, with just a word.

One Little Lunch

Mark 6, John 6

Jesus and his twelve disciples traveled all over the land teaching about God's love. Crowds of people came to hear what the wise teacher Jesus had to say. But this kept Jesus and his disciples so busy that they rarely had time to rest.

"Come," Jesus told them one day. "Let us go to a place far from the crowds, where we may rest awhile."

Jesus and his disciples took a boat across Lake Galilee. But someone had seen them set sail. The word spread about where Jesus was going. When Jesus and his disciples got to the shore on the other side, a huge crowd had already gathered on the hillside.

Jesus and his disciples were tired, but Jesus wanted to help people. He saw how much these people wanted to learn from him and to hear what he had to say. So Jesus shared lessons with them, and he told them stories of his Father's love.

The people would not leave Jesus's side.

As the sun began to set, the disciples knew that the people must be getting hungry. "Jesus," one of the disciples said to him, "it is getting late. These people have nothing to eat. And there is no food here. We should tell them to go. If we send them away now, they might have time to reach a nearby town to buy food."

"Why don't *we* feed them?" Jesus asked. He turned to one of the disciples. "Philip, where can we buy enough bread to feed these people?"

Philip looked at the crowd gathered on the hillside. There had to be five thousand or more people there! He shook his head. "It would take me a year to save enough money to feed all of these people! And even then, the food I could afford would only be enough for everyone to get just a pinch of bread."

Where Philip saw a problem, Jesus saw a chance to show people the power of God.

Andrew, another one of Jesus's disciples, had been searching the crowd for food. He walked up to Jesus with a boy by his side. "This boy has five loaves of bread and two small fish," Andrew said. "But that's not enough to feed even a handful of people."

Jesus just smiled and said, "Ask everyone to sit down."

The disciples walked throughout the grassy hill, asking the people to sit.

The people grew quiet as Jesus took the little boy's basket in his hands. They listened as he prayed.

"Father, thank you for this food. We are grateful that what you give is always enough."

Jesus broke the bread, dividing the loaves among the disciples. Then Jesus broke the fish and divided the pieces among them.

"Now," he said to his disciples, "give everyone here some bread and fish. Make sure that *everyone* is fed."

The disciples looked down at the food they held in their hands. They saw the small, broken loaves of bread and the

tiny, broken pieces of fish. Then they looked out at the sea of people spread across the hillside. The disciples had no idea how Jesus planned to feed them all. But they trusted him.

The disciples walked into the crowd and began to serve the people. Everyone wondered how long it would be before they ran out of food. The people watched the disciples and wondered if a miracle was about to take place. They had heard about how Jesus had worked miracles in the past.

Somehow, every time a person reached for food, it was there. The people ate and ate. And somehow, everyone ate until they were full. Before long, more than five thousand people had been fed.

When Jesus saw that everyone had eaten, he told his disciples, "Now, go and gather all of the leftover food. We don't want any to go to waste."

The disciples each took a basket. Then they walked throughout the crowd that was spread across the hill. They gathered any food that was left, placing it in the baskets as Jesus had told them to do. Even after feeding the entire crowd, they were left with twelve baskets full of food!

The disciples were amazed. Five thousand people had seen the boy's five loaves and two small fish. And five thousand people had seen Jesus feed everyone with the gift of one little lunch, with only a simple blessing. It was a miracle that Jesus had fed all of those people, and they knew that Jesus was a great Prophet.

With that, the disciples set out again across the lake. And
Jesus went up on the mountain to rest and pray.

Now I See

One day, Jesus and his disciples were traveling through the city of Jerusalem. As they were walking, they passed a blind man.

One of the disciples turned to Jesus. He asked, "Teacher, someone must have sinned to make this man blind. Was it him? Or was it his parents?"

Jesus answered, "Neither this man nor his parents sinned. He was born blind. God made him this way so that he could be an example of the power of God."

"Who's there?" the blind man asked, reaching in front of him.

Jesus took the man's hands. "My name is Jesus." Jesus knelt down in front of the man and picked up some dirt. Then he spit into the dirt and mixed it together to make mud. He gently spread the mud onto the blind man's eyes.

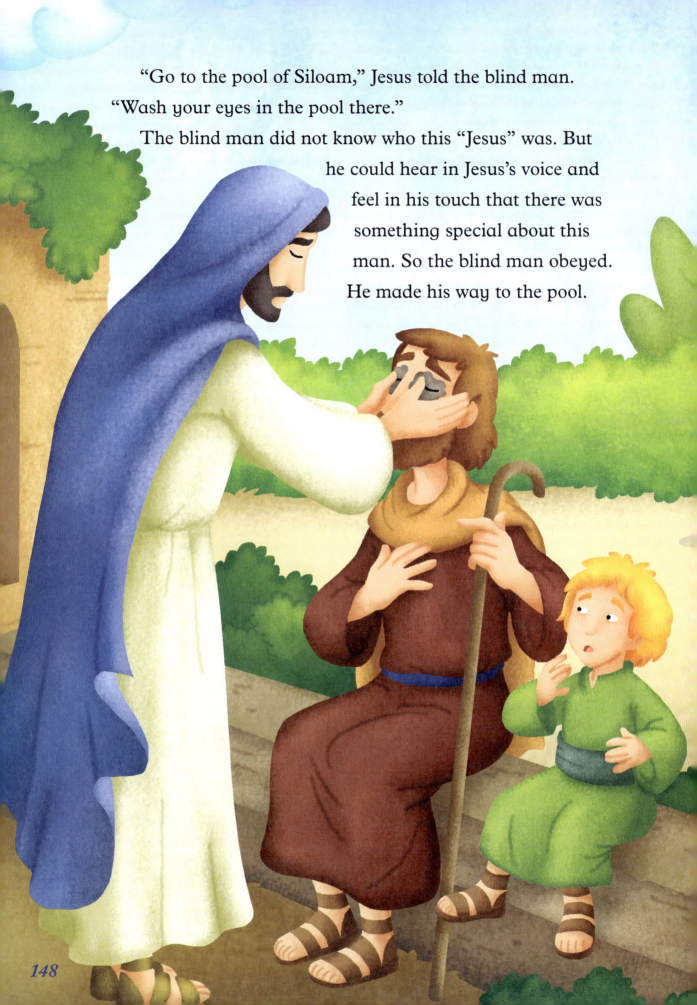

"Go to the pool of Siloam," Jesus told the blind man. "Wash your eyes in the pool there."

The blind man did not know who this "Jesus" was. But he could hear in Jesus's voice and feel in his touch that there was something special about this man. So the blind man obeyed. He made his way to the pool.

Once there, he washed the mud off his eyes. Then, for the first time in his life, light and colors flooded his vision. He could see!

The once-blind man was overjoyed. He walked around, looking at everything as he went. He was amazed at all of the wonderful sights—the children smiling, the green trees swaying, the ripe fruits in the marketplace. There was so much to see!

Local people knew of the blind man. So when they saw him laughing and looking around, they began to whisper.

"Isn't that the man who was blind?" one person asked.

"Wasn't he the beggar?" someone else asked.

Some people replied, "Yes, that is him."

But others answered, "No, that is not him. It only looks like him."

The man overheard people talking. He said, "It is true! I was the blind man you saw begging in the streets. But now I can see!"

The people looked at him in wonder.

"How?" someone asked. "How can you see now after all these years?"

The man answered, "Jesus made some mud and rubbed it on my eyes. He told me to wash in the pool of Siloam. So I did. And after I washed, I could see!"

"Where is this Jesus?" the people asked.

But the man did not know.

Over the next few days, the man's story spread across the land. Powerful religious leaders known as the Pharisees heard about this miracle. And they heard that Jesus was being named as the one who had healed him.

The Pharisees had heard of Jesus's miracles before. They had even heard people say that Jesus was God's Son. But the Pharisees did not believe that this ordinary man could really have been sent from God. They wanted to find something wrong with Jesus. They wanted to prove that he was not godly—and that he was an ordinary man. They also wanted to stop everyone from talking about him.

First, the Pharisees questioned the once-blind man's parents. "Is this your son, the one who you say was born blind? How can he now see?"

His parents were afraid that what they said would get them in trouble, so they answered carefully. "Well, we know that this is our son. And we know that he was born blind. But we don't know how he got his sight or who gave it to him. Ask him. He is old enough to tell you what happened."

Then the Pharisees turned to the once-blind man. "Honor God by telling the truth. Who healed you? It could not have been Jesus because Jesus is just an ordinary man."

The man whom Jesus healed answered, "Whether he is ordinary or not, I do not know. I know one thing: I was blind, and now I can see."

The Pharisees said, "We don't know who this man Jesus is or where he came from."

"How can a man do something so wonderful, so amazing, and yet you don't know where he came from?" the man said. "He healed me! Only God's power can do that!"

The once-blind man believed that Jesus was sent from God. But the Pharisees still did not believe. And they knew that the man had been telling this story all over town. This made them really mad. The Pharisees threw the man out into the streets.

Jesus heard about how the Pharisees had treated the man. So Jesus went to go check on him.

"Are you okay?" Jesus asked him.

The man froze. He immediately recognized Jesus's voice. And for the first time, the man looked into the eyes of the person who had healed him.

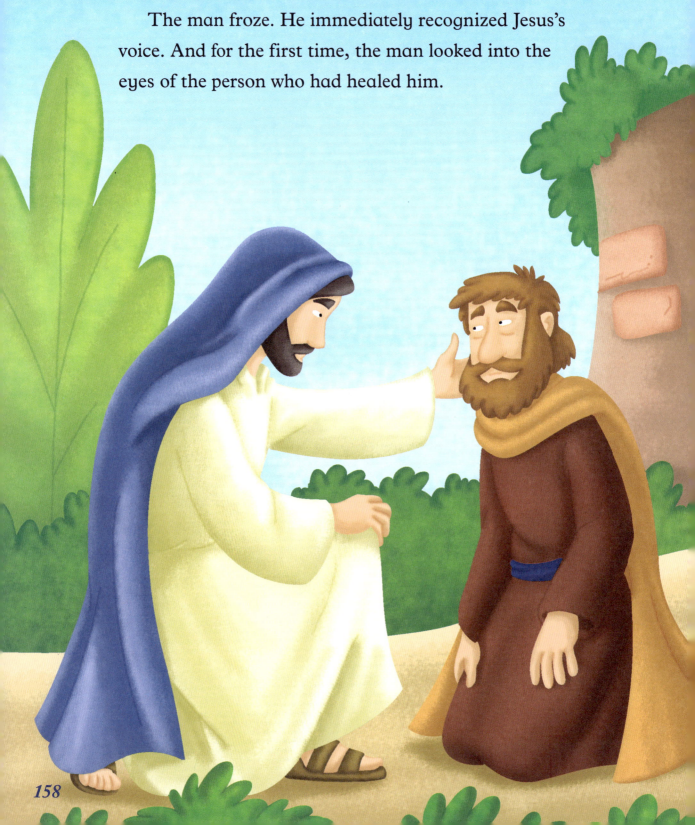

Jesus then said to him, "Do you believe in the Son of God?"

"Please, Lord, tell me who he is so that I can believe in him," the man replied.

"You have seen him with your own eyes," Jesus said. "It is the man who speaks to you now."

The man fell to his knees and said, "Lord, I believe."
Jesus smiled. With one healing touch he had brought one
more person to believe in him.

Even after all of Jesus's miracles, the Pharisees did not
believe that Jesus was the Son of God. But with just one
miracle, the blind man believed.

Who Is My Neighbor?

Luke 10

People across the land kept talking about this man named Jesus. They talked about his teachings and his miracles and that maybe he was even the Son of God. Jesus seemed to know so much about God's Word. And he talked about God as if he knew God in a special way. People often came from miles around just to hear Jesus teach and to learn more about God and his Word.

One day, Jesus was sharing God's Word with a group of people. There was a man listening who had studied God's Word all of his life. He asked Jesus, "Teacher, I want to live forever with God. What do I have to do to make sure that happens?"

"What does God's Word say?" Jesus asked him.

The man smiled. He had this part of God's Word memorized. "It says to love God with all of your heart, all of your soul, all of your strength, and all of your mind," the man answered. "It also says to love your neighbor as yourself."

"That's right," Jesus said. "Do all of this, and you will have eternal life."

"I know how to love God fully," the man said. "But who is my neighbor?"

This time, Jesus answered the man with a story.

"Once, a Jewish man was traveling on the road from Jerusalem to Jericho. Some bad men attacked him. They took his clothes, his money, and his supplies. Then they beat him up and ran away. They left the man on the side of the road.

"The man was so badly hurt that he couldn't walk. Soon after, a Jewish priest came by and saw the man lying there. *How horrible!* the priest thought. But the priest didn't want any trouble. So, instead of helping the man, the priest crossed to the other side of the road to stay far away from him.

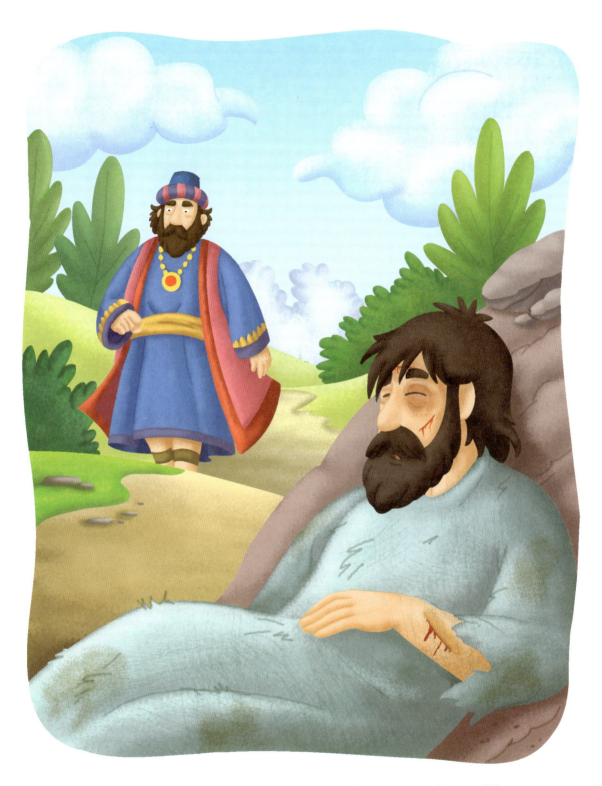

"Next, a Jewish man called a Levite came along. He, too, saw the hurt man lying on the side of the road. But he didn't want to take the time to stop. And he, too, crossed to the other side of the road.

"Finally, a man from Samaria came walking down the road. He saw that the man was badly hurt. The Samaritan knew that the hurt man was probably Jewish. And he knew that Jewish people and Samaritan people didn't usually get along. People would probably even make fun of him for just speaking with a Jewish man. But the Samaritan still wanted to help the man.

"He knelt at
the man's side and pulled
out some supplies from his bag.
He carefully cleaned the man's cuts and gently
bandaged the man's wounds.

169

"Then the Samaritan lifted the beaten man onto his own donkey and brought him to an inn.

"The Samaritan paid for the man to have a room at the inn. He cared for the man throughout the night. The next morning, he left the man at the inn so that he could rest and heal. He even gave money to the innkeeper, telling him, 'Here is some extra money for this man. Please take care of him. If you need more money than this for his care, please care for him, and I will pay you back when I return.'"

When Jesus finished the story, he turned to the man who had asked, "Who is my neighbor?" Jesus asked him, "Now, which of these three men—the priest, the Levite, or the Samaritan—acted like a neighbor to the man who was attacked?"

Even though the man had studied God's Word, this was not an easy question for him to answer. He knew that the priest and the Levite were both Jewish and that they were both people of God. He knew they *should* have helped the hurt man, but they didn't. And the Samaritan? At that time, Jews and Samaritans didn't get along—at all. So the last person anyone would expect to help a hurt Jewish man on the side of the road would be a Samaritan. Yet the Samaritan was the only one who stopped to help.

In his heart, the man knew the answer to Jesus's question. The crowd listened as the man said, "The person who showed the man mercy is the one who is his neighbor."

Jesus nodded. Then he said, "Go and do the same for your neighbor."

With that simple story, the man who knew so much about God's Word learned a new and very important lesson: God's people shouldn't only be kind to those who are kind to them. And God's people shouldn't only be nice to people who look the same or talk the same as they do. Everyone should be a neighbor to everyone else. God's people should always show God's love to all.

Jesus Is Alive!

Matthew 27–28, Mark 15–16, Luke 23–24, John 19–20

Jesus spent a lot of time with his followers. And he often told them that he would one day give up his life as part of God's plan so that everyone who believes in him would be saved. He told his followers that he would soon die. But he also told them that he would rise from death and see them again.

At the time, many of Jesus's followers did not understand what he meant. But they would see for themselves how Jesus would give up his life to save us all.

After Jesus died on a cross, there was a powerful earthquake. The ground beneath the people shook. Trees swayed. The rocks split in two. And total darkness fell across the land.

Many people did not believe that Jesus was the true Son of God. But many others *did* believe. And many more came to believe after they felt the earth move that day.

Jesus's death is not the end of the story. In fact, it is only the beginning. Soon, all over the world, people would hear about Jesus.

They would learn about the Son of God who came to save the world.

That evening, after Jesus died, his body was taken down from the cross. Then a man named Joseph, one of Jesus's followers, carefully wrapped his body in fine linen and laid it in a tomb. Two of Jesus's followers—Mary the mother of James, and Mary Magdalene—silently watched as Jesus's body was placed in the tomb. Then Joseph rolled a huge rock in front of the tomb to keep Jesus's body safe.

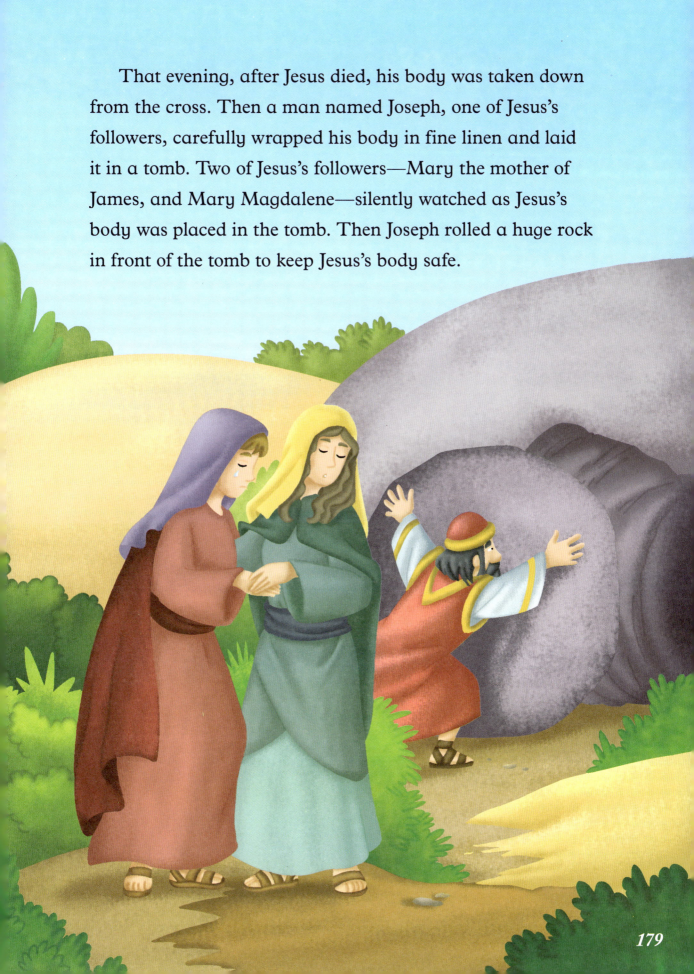

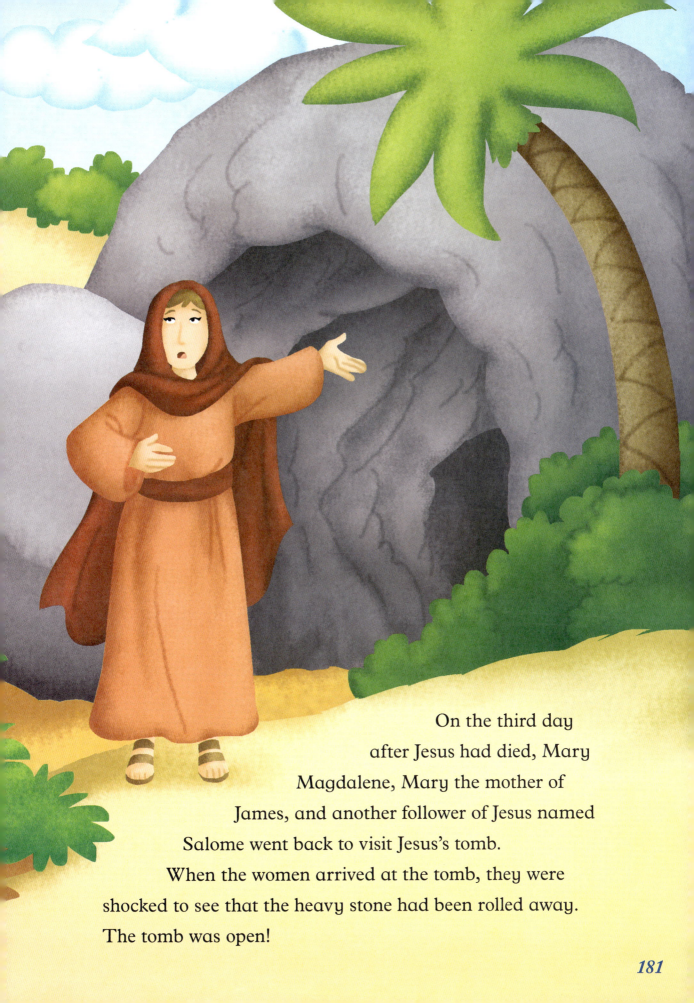

On the third day
after Jesus had died, Mary
Magdalene, Mary the mother of
James, and another follower of Jesus named
Salome went back to visit Jesus's tomb.
When the women arrived at the tomb, they were
shocked to see that the heavy stone had been rolled away.
The tomb was open!

The three women tiptoed toward the tomb and peeked in the entrance. There, sitting inside, was a young man—an angel! His face shined like a bright light. And his clothes were glowing white. But they didn't see Jesus anywhere.

The three women were too frightened to move any farther.

"Don't be afraid," the angel said. "You're looking for Jesus, but he is not here. He is risen!"

Could this be true? Mary Magdalene wondered.

Could Jesus really have risen from the dead? Mary the mother of James thought.

Salome shook her head in disbelief. *Could Jesus truly be alive?*

"Go," the man told them. "Tell the disciples that Jesus is risen. They will see him again—just as he said they would."

The women did as the angel told them to do. They ran to tell Jesus's disciples the news.

Jesus wanted to show all of his disciples that he was real. He wanted them to know that he really had risen to life again, as he had promised. . . .

Later that day, Jesus appeared beside two of his followers while they were walking down the road.

After that, he came to the house where the disciples had gathered. Jesus talked and ate dinner with his disciples. They were so surprised and happy to see Jesus. All of Jesus's disciples were at the dinner—except for the disciple named Thomas.

Thomas hadn't yet seen Jesus for himself. When the others told Thomas about seeing Jesus, Thomas had a hard time believing the news.

"When I can see and touch and feel his scars for myself," Thomas told the other disciples, "only then will I believe that Jesus is alive."

A week later, Jesus appeared again. This time, all of the disciples were together.

"Peace to you all," Jesus said. Then he turned to Thomas and said, "Look, Thomas. See these scars? Touch them, feel them, and believe."

Thomas was stunned. He opened his eyes and reached out his hand.

"My Lord and my God!" he cried. Finally, Thomas believed that Jesus was alive.

"You believe only because you have seen me," Jesus said. "Blessed are those who don't see me and yet still believe."

For forty days after Jesus had risen, he spent time with his disciples and spoke with hundreds of people. But then it was time for Jesus to go back home to be with God. Before Jesus left, he gave all of his followers a very important mission.

"Go and teach the whole world about me and my Father,"
Jesus told them. "Teach them all of the things I have taught
you. And remember, I am with you always and forever."

Before Jesus was taken up to heaven, he blessed his followers. Jesus promised that he would send the Holy Spirit to help us and teach us what is true and that the Holy Spirit would always be with us.

Jesus's followers spread the Word of God. They went out into the world and told the story of Jesus.

Those who believe in Jesus today are *still* doing what Jesus told his followers to do so many years ago. They are telling everyone about their Savior so that the whole world learns about God's offer of love and forgiveness to us all.